The Real Treasure

A folktale from Kazakhstan

adapted by Walton Burns

textinspector.com

© 2020 Alphabet Publishing.
ISBN: 978-1-948492-89-8
All rights reserved.
Illustrations by Kamil Sawczuk.
Map created by Central Intelligence Agency, 2003, Public Domain

For discounts on class sets, contact us:
Alphabet Publishing • 1024 Main St. #172
Branford, CT 06405 • USA
info@alphabetpublishingbooks.com
www.alphabetpublishingbooks.com

Table of Contents

About the Story	4
The Most Precious Treasure	5
Vocabulary	17
Questions	18
Creating	19
Learn More	20
Other Graded Reader Titles	23

About the story

Before you read

For a long time, in Kazakhstan, many people lived as **nomads**. Nomads do not live in one place. They do not build stone or wood houses and they do not live in towns. Instead they move around. This helps them find food for their animals.

The Kazakh nomads traveled north in the summer. They went away from hot places. They found cool places with green grass. In the winter, they traveled south. They went away from the snow. They found grass for cows and horses to eat. Because they traveled a lot, Kazakhs lived in round tents called **yurts**. You can take a yurt down. You can travel with it. Some people still live in these houses.

Nomads in Kazakhstan and all over the world still travel to find food. They live in tents or houses that can move. Would you like to be a nomad?

What would be the biggest change in your life?

A long time ago, there was a young man from Kazakhstan
His name was Bakyt.
That means "happy" in Kazakh.
But he was always unhappy.

Bakyt always wanted more.
He wanted a bigger house.
He wanted more food for dinner.
His horse was too small.
His sword was too weak.

So Bakyt's father took him to Mergen.

Mergen was an old man.

He was very wise.

Can you guess what Mergen means?

Mergen asked Bakyt, "Why are you sad?"
"I want to be rich," Bakyt said,
"I want beautiful things.
Expensive things."

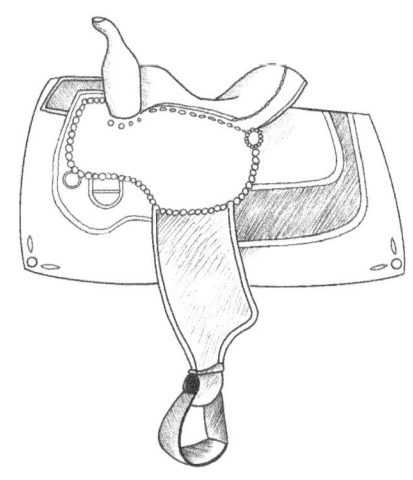

"Very well," said Mergen,
"Sell me your eyes.
I will give you a beautiful saddle for your horse."
Bakyt said, "But wise Mergen,
if I sell you my eyes, I cannot ride.
Then I do not need a beautiful saddle."

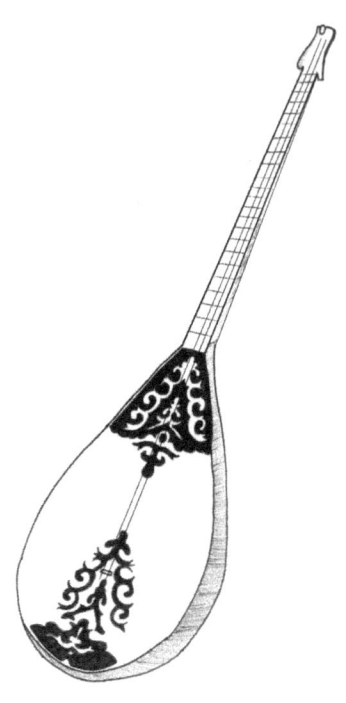

"Very well," said Mergen,
"Then sell me your ears.
I will give you a golden dombra."
Bakyt said, "But wise Mergen,
if I sell you my ears,
I will not need a dombra."

"Then sell me your nose.
I will give you delicious food."
Bakyt said, "But wise Mergen,
without a nose,
the food will not smell delicious.
It will not taste good."

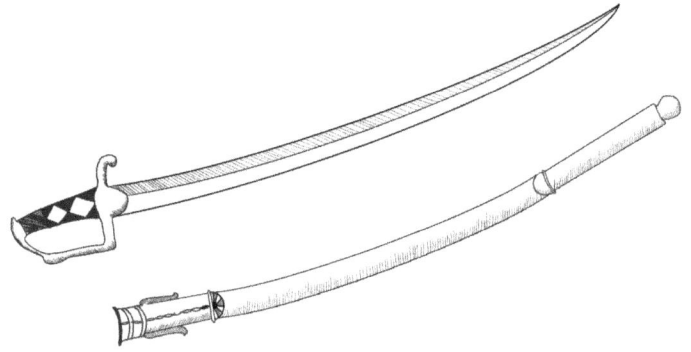

"Then sell me your arms.
I will give you an exquisite sword."
Bakyt said, "But wise Mergen,
if I sell you my arms,
I cannot use a sword."

"Then sell me your legs.
I will give you a fast horse."
Bakyt said, "If I give you my legs,
I cannot ride a horse."

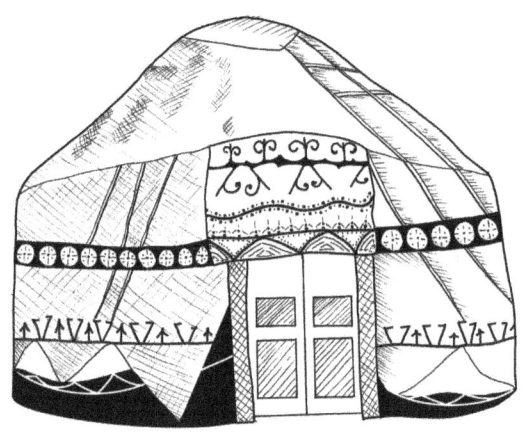

"What about this?" said Mergen,
"Sell me your heart.
I will give you an enormous yurt."
Bakyt said, "But wise Mergen,
if I sell you my heart, I will die.
I will not need a yurt to live in."

"Your body is healthy and whole.
Your family loves you.
You have a home and food to eat," said Mergen,
"These are the real treasures.
Enjoy what you have. Do not ask for more."

Bakyt went back home.

He never complained again.

Sometimes, he even smiled!

Vocabulary

delicious: tastes good

enormous: large, big

exquisite: very beautiful

Kazakh: a group of people who live in Kazakhstan. They have lived there a long time. It is also the name of the language the people speak.

treasure: something that costs a lot of money or something that is important

wise: knowing about the best way to live

Questions

1. Why was Bakyt unhappy?

2. Why did his parents take him to Mergen?

3. What does "mergen" mean in Kazakh?

4. Mergen teaches Bakyt to be happy. How does he do that?

5. What do you think of Mergen's advice?

6. Would you take any of Mergen's offers?

7. Do you agree people should be happy with what they have? Or should people try to get more and more?

8. Kazakh people are nomads. What parts of the story show this?

Creating

Do you know a story like this from your culture? Perhaps it's a story about a young person who is never happy. Maybe you know a story about a wise person who gives advice about life.

Tell the story to the class or write it down.

You may also want to create your own story!

Learn More

Kazakhstan is a country with a long and rich history. You can learn more about it from online resources, such as the Simple Wikipedia article at https://simple.wikipedia.org/wiki/Kazakhstan.

THE CAUCASUS AND CENTRAL ASIA

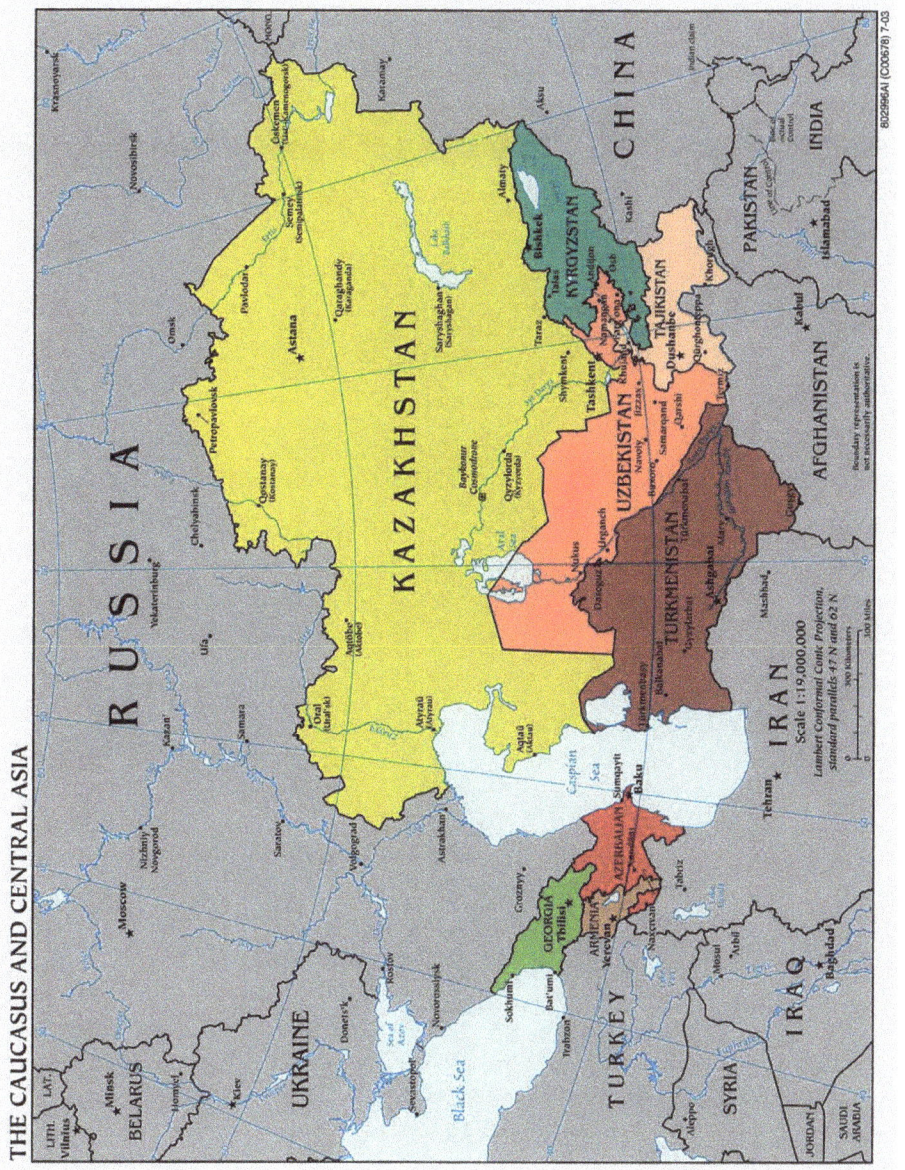

This map is from 2003. The capital of Kazakhstan was renamed Nur-Sultan in 2019.

Other Graded Reader Titles

The Feast that Stopped a War

The Wise Little Girl

How Babik Cheated Death

The Fox and the Magpie

The Freedom Bird

www.AlphabetPublish.Com/Readers

Leveling information	
Word Count	341
Word Tokens	119
Avg. Words/Sentence	8.05
Gunning Fog	4.49
Fleisch- Kincaid Reading Ease	92.31
Fleisch-Kincaid Grade	2.38

all leveling done with textinspector.com